# Magnificent Peacocks

Christina Rose

# MAGNIFICENT PEACOCKS COLOURING BOOK
Beautiful birds and perfect plumes.  Anti-stress colouring.

ISBN: 978-1-912511-72-3

Created by Christina Rose

Images under licence from Shutterstock

 BELL & MACKENZIE
PUBLISHING LIMITED
www.bellmackenzie.com

Beauty has so many forms.

Be like a peacock and dance
with all of your beauty.
Debasish Mridha

It dances today, my heart,
like a peacock it dances.
Rabindranath Tagore

The future belongs to those
who believe in the beauty
of their dreams.
Eleanor Roosevelt

The pride of the peacock
is the glory of god

Peace is the beauty of life.

A beautiful thing is never perfect.

I shall always remember how
the peacocks' tails shimmered
when the moon rose amongst
the tall trees.
Hermann Hesse

If you foolishly ignore
beauty, then you will soon
find yourself without it.

Peacocks symbolise new begin-
nings & eternal life

Everything has beauty, but
not everyone sees it.
Confucius

There is no exquisite beauty
without some strangeness in
the proportion.

Edgar Allan Poe

A thing of beauty is a joy forever:
Its loveliness increases; it will
never pass into nothingness.
John Keats

Life is not measured by the
number of breaths we take,
but by the moments that
take our breath away

Dream tonight of peacock tails,
Diamond fields and spouter
whales. Ills are many, blessing
few, But dreams tonight will
shelter you.

Herman Melville

 I do not believe that any peacock envies another peacock his tail, because every peacock is persuaded that his own tail is the finest in the world.

John Ruskin

Many a peacock hides his
peacock tail from all eyes
- and calls it his pride.
Friedrich Nietzsche

Though we travel the
world over to find the
beautiful, we must carry it
with us or we find it not.
Ralph Waldo Emerson

Beauty of whatever kind, in
its supreme development,
invariably excites the
sensitive soul to tears.
Edgar Allan Poe

Beauty is unbearable,
drives us to despair,
offering us for a minute the
glimpse of an eternity that
we should like to stretch
out over the whole of time.
Albert Camus

There is nothing that makes
its way more directly to the
soul than beauty.
Joseph Addison

Beauty is the shadow of
God on the universe.
Gabriela Mistral

Anyone who keeps the
ability to see beauty never
grows old.

Franz Kafka

Treasure the magnificent.

The most beautiful gift of nature is that it gives one pleasure to look around and try to comprehend what we see.

Albert Einstein

Nature never hurries. Atom
by atom, little by little, she
achieves her work.
Ralph Waldo Emerson

Those who contemplate
the beauty of the earth find
reserves of strength that
will endure as long as life
lasts.

Rachel Carson

Tell me, sir.
Have you ever heard
A peacock sing?
Hold your ear
To this mystical stone
And you will hear
Sacred hymns flowing
To the vibrations
Of the perfumed
Wind.

Suzy Kassem

One touch of nature makes
the whole world kin.
William Shakespeare

If you truly love Nature, you
will find beauty everywhere.
Vincent Van Gogh

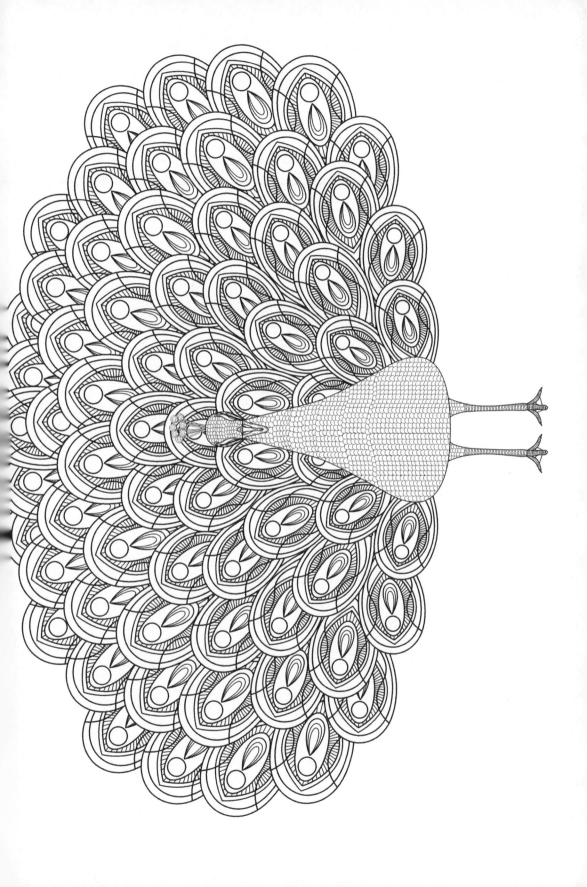

Those who find beauty
in all of nature will find
themselves at one with the
secrets of life itself.

L. Wolfe Gilbert

Nature always wears the
colours of the spirit.

Ralph Waldo Emerson

The beauty of the natural
world lies in the details.

Natalie Angier

In all things of nature there is
something of the marvelous.
Aristotle

Those who contemplate
the beauty of the Earth find
reserves of strength that
will endure as long as life
lasts.

Rachel Carson

I believe the world is
incomprehensibly beautiful
an endless prospect of magic
and wonder.

Ansel Adams

Looking at beauty in the
world is the first step of
purifying the mind.
Amit Ray

Beauty awakens the soul to act.
Dante Alighieri

Beauty in things exists in the
mind which contemplates
them.
David Hume

The soul that sees beauty may sometimes walk alone.

Johann Wolfgang von Goethe

The beautiful is always bizarre.
Charles Baudelaire

Do not try to dissect the
beauty of a rainbow.

Butterflies come to pretty flowers.

Every atom is a magnificent glow.

There is certainly no absolute standard of beauty. That precisely is what makes its pursuit so interesting.

John Kenneth Galbraith

Peacock dreams are beautiful